TABLE OF CONTENTS

CHAPTER 1:

The Marriage Basics

When it comes to getting married, only a few people are sure what they are getting themselves into. We have our hopes, expectations, and dreams of what marriage indeed looks like. When we watch some of the movies starts, we like, we think that the kinds of weddings they show on TV are what it is like in real life. Let me tell you something. You have no idea what marriage is until you are there!

Here Are some of the Secrets I Can Tell You Will Strengthen Your Marriage if You Pay Attention to Them;

Secret 1 Marriage Is more about Intimacy than Sex

If you ask anyone that is single and planning to get married what marriage is about, they will tell you it is about sex.

While there is so much value you draw from getting married to your partner as far as your sexual relationship, the truth is that a good marriage is built on intimacy. This is the only route you are going to enjoy good sex and not the other way around.

Secret 2 Marriage Uncovers Self-Centeredness but Also Cultivates Selflessness

Confessions, I didn't realize how selfish I was until I got married to my wife. One year down the line, my selfishness was out in the light. I could choose what restaurant we would eat, who gets to clean up, what movie we will watch, and who gets the remote. It was even shocking that each time we argued, my wife would apologize first even if I was the one at fault.

Learn to place your spouse's needs before your own if you are going to make it last. This is how you start learning the true meaning of being selfless. Trust me, even though this is a hard lesson to learn, it is a beautiful reminder of God's selflessness when He gave His all so that you and I can have it all in abundance.

Secret 3 Oneness Means Being one

The truth is, when we get into marriage, we stop being "me" and become "us." We stop having things that are "mine," and we view everything as "ours." You have to care for everything as though they were not just yours but also belonged to the person you love most.

Secret 4 At Certain Points, You Will Be disappointed

This is one of the most challenging realities that most couples find it hard to believe. You must be aware of your spouse's humanity and yours too. However, it is interesting that this reality does not hit home sooner until you are disappointed. You must choose to embrace the grace of God so that every hurt and wound pave the way for forgiveness and restoration. Each injury should serve as a constant reminder of our need to love profoundly and better each time.

Secret 5 You Must Learn the Meaning of Forgiveness whether You Like It or Not

The fact that you will get hurt means that you have to embrace the reality of learning the essence of forgiveness.

One lesson that you must know is that forgiveness comes not just because your partner deserves it but also because it whelms from a heart that understands how much forgiveness we had received even when we least deserved it.

Secret 6 Marriage Will Cost You

When you are in the glory of marriage, the truth is that you will lose a part of yourself. In other words, you exchange a portion of who you are for the sake of taking up a little bit of who your partner is. In short, you learn the essence of giving and taking. In marriage, you know to let go of the things that do not matter to you at all. Eventually, you realize that what you have given is far much less than what you ultimately receive.

Trust me; love is good, just like that!

Secret 7 Love Is a Series of Decision and Not a Feeling

Before you got married, the chances are that you did not understand the intense feelings that you felt. Suddenly, you start realizing that you cannot trust your feelings because there are days when you don't like your spouse, and most days, you just can't let him go.

The actual test of love is what you do when you feel that you don't like your spouse. Understand that marriage is about choosing to love your partner even when you don't want to. You are choosing to give your all into serving them because you committed to them, the world, and God that you would love them "for better or for worse." It is about you always choosing your spouse instead of yourself. That is what real life means!

Secret 8 Marriage Requires that You Learn how to Communicate

We have mentioned before that one of the essential building blocks of marriage is compelling, transparent, and honest communication. What matters the most is what you would do about it. How will you choose to communicate to them how you feel?

In short, marriage is about you continue communicating with your spouse, your values, beliefs, opinions, and feelings. It is about not fearing to ask the tough questions, tell the hard truth, or even respond to difficult problems. It serves as a lifeline between you and your spouse.

Secret 9 Marriage Is Not the end of Your Destination

When you are still dating, it is often easy to look at marriage as your grand finale! It is that thing that you have been dreaming about since you were a little girl or boy. It is what you have lived for all your life, and finally, it is here. The following thing you think of when you get married is, "Now what?"

The truth is that your purpose and passion will supersede the relationship you have with your partner. God will use your relationship and the love between you and your spouse for the glory of His name. Your marriage is not the end of everything. Instead, it is just the beginning of the many more blessings he has in store for you.

Secret 10 Marriage Offers You a Glimpse of So Much more

God has so much more in store for you. Realize that there is a reason why God uses the institution of marriage when talking about the love He has for the church.

There is no single relationship you will have that will compare to that intimacy exchanged through marriage here on earth. In other words, it is through marriage that God keeps making us be more of Him.

CHAPTER 2:

Communication

Ensuring that you have open communication with your partner will help you build a long-lasting and happy relationship. By contrast, people with poor communication skills are much more likely to have unresolved fights and unhealthy relationships.

Self-Disclosure

We get scared when we think about sharing or revealing a secret about ourselves. This triggers feelings of guilt, shame, and fear. When you share the vulnerabilities with a stranger or someone you don't know very well, this can potentially lead to more insecurities.

Without meaning to, the other person can challenge our core beliefs, which can trigger anxiety or depression.

Sharing your vulnerability with your closest friends or your partner can be liberating, and it's a great way to strengthen your bond.

Rewards of Self-Disclosure

Self-disclosure can lead to long-lasting relationships, reduced anxiety, and elimination of the feeling of abandonment. Some of the many benefits of self-disclosure are listed below.

- **Eliminate feelings of guilt** — Chronic feelings of guilt can change a person's entire life. But keeping all the parts of yourself that you feel ashamed of hidden is impossible to sustain. Remember that imperfections are a part of life, and when you start hiding things from the people you love, you will begin the ensuing of shame and guilt can take over your whole life.

- **Improve communication** — When you open up to your partner, chances are you will inspire them to do the same. This will naturally lead to better communication between you. Make an effort to share your true self with your partner. You will find yourself sharing the most intimate details about your life and living happily together in no time.

- **More intimate relationships** — Disclosing personal information and sharing your feelings will help you form closer bonds with the people you love.

This will lead to more meaningful interactions with those around you. Indeed, a welcome change from the unsatisfying and shallow relationship you might have had in the past.

- **Increased self-knowledge** — We're all pretty well-aware of all the secrets we keep. So, you might be wondering how sharing them with your partner can increase knowledge about yourself. The truth is, when you don't share your feelings with anyone, you tend to make assumptions that have no real basis in facts. Moreover, going over and over your secrets in your mind will never provide you with any total closure. Sharing this information with your partner will give you a new and fresh perspective, and you will be eager to find out even more information that can help you solve these issues.

Listening Skills

Listening skills are probably the most crucial step to bridge the communication gap between you and your partner. When someone feels indeed heard, they tend to feel empowered, loved, supported, and understood. Your listening skill is essential if you want your partner to feel loved and cared for.

But before we talk about something called "active listening," which is our goal, we need to show you the difference between really listening and pseudo-listening.

Pseudo-Listening vs. Real Listening

Pseudo-listening is a concept that we should all be aware of. As you may have guessed, pseudo-listening is only half-listening to what the other person says, not paying much attention. One sign of pseudo-listening is when you start thinking about how to reply to what the other person is saying before they're done talking. Another is when you engage in other activities, such as looking at your phone when talking. This can lead to many issues since people who have this habit have trouble keeping successful relationships. They're unable to fully process the information that other people share with them, which can be harmful to the relationship. Not feeling heard might also trigger feelings of anxiety in someone with fearful or preoccupied attachment styles.

Listening Blocks

Numerous things can hinder your capacity to remain focused on what the other person is trying to say to you. Suppose you've even been in that situation yourself. In that case, you probably remember that your attention was mostly focused on what you were going to say about yourself than what other people were saying. Maybe you practiced your speech in your mind over and over to avoid making mistakes, or we just too anxious about speaking publicly. Whatever the cause, listening blocks can only have a damaging effect on your relationship.

Active Listening

If you feel that your communication skills require some work and improve your relationships, you need to listen to your daily routine actively. Knowing about pseudo-listening and listening blocks is an excellent first step, but good communication requires additional work.

When you start to listen to other people truly, you will be able to respond more insightfully, in a way that makes them feel you dully support them.

Step 1: Paraphrasing

Paraphrasing is expressing the meaning of what someone else has said using different words. A practical example might help to make the concept clearer.

Person A: I don't think my partner cares about me anymore. They never reply to my messages or calls anymore.

Person B: So, you feel neglected because your partner isn't talking to you as often as they used to?

In paraphrasing, you use your own words to help you focus on what the other person is saying and to show that you understand the meaning they're trying to convey.

Step 2: Clarifying

Consider clarifying as an addition to paraphrasing. In this step, you will ask questions until you understand what the other person is trying to communicate. Look at the example above once more. Notice how Person B not only paraphrased Person A's statement but also turned it into a question? This is the idea behind clarification.

With this process, you will gather more information and know what message the other person conveys.

Step 3: Feedback

The third and final step is providing feedback. After you fully absorb and comprehend the information presented to you, it's time to share your thoughts. Once you have assimilated their words, you offer a message back, communicating that you have listened to the speaker and want to engage in a meaningful dialogue.

The key to providing meaningful feedback is to offer a message free of judgment. When the speaker receives positive feedback from you, they know that you understand their side of the story and feel empowered. This will also lead to less anxiety in the relationship. There are three basic rules you should follow when giving feedback. The feedback should be honest (even if it's painful), it should be immediate, and it should have a supportive tone.

Expressing Your Needs

Expressing your needs may seem like an easy thing to do, but it can be complicated. Many people just aren't used to asking for attention or saying their needs. Yet others may think they don't need anything from other people. The prominent problem people face is that we have become more alienated from the concept of expressing our needs. Many people have probably gone years without it. We might get the urge to communicate our needs to our friends, family members, or romantic partner, but we often smother and ignore it. This is most likely because we fear rejection, which could increase the problems in the relationship.

CHAPTER 3:

Intimacy

Things may start to feel a bit dull, and sex drives may not be as strong as they used to be. Give time for a sexual relationship with your partner by trying new things, communicating about personal desires, and playing fun games.

Increase Couple Intimacy

When you become progressively more comfortable with someone, it can take away some of the mystery. This is because there is no longer the excitement of getting to know a person, and having everything you do together be brand new. At the beginning of a relationship, you are eager to have sex with each other because the other person is unique and hot and a novelty of sorts. As you get used to them, it can be easy to lose those feelings and settle into the comfortability of everything (like their body or your routine). Getting to this point in your relationship is fun and comforting in its way, and is different from, but in some ways better than, the early stages. From a sexual perspective, though, we don't want the coming of this stage of your relationship to bring with it the end of exciting sex life.

If you are a long-term or married couple, you have likely tried every one of the classic sex positions together from missionary to 69. You have probably also developed a routine of your favorite parts and the order in which you do them by now.

Start having sex casually before getting together romantically, or you may have begun having sex when you became a couple. Either way, the beginning of any relationship comes with a lot of uncharted territories. You are exploring a new person's entire body- inside and out, and letting them see all of yours. Of course, this can be nerve-wracking. There will be some positions and sexual activities that you won't be entirely comfortable doing with this person yet, even if you have done them before with someone else. There are certain positions you can stick to that are more comfortable at the beginning of a relationship, and that is best for getting to know someone's body and what they like. These positions serve us well when we are newly having sex with a person and are looking for the best way to help each other orgasm. This stage of discovery, however, is something that we want to return to every so often. We want to rediscover the person's body and what they like as if it is the first time, we explore it. People's desires change, and their bodies change. It is vital to continue to know how to pleasure your partner as they grow and change, and to expect the same from them for yourself.

Importance of Spicing Up Your Sex Life

The primary importance of spicing up your sex life is to increase intimacy between you and your partner. Not only does this help your sex life become more fun and exciting, but it also improves the communication and bond between you and your partner.

We will look at how you can maintain intimacy with your partner and achieve a greater intimacy level and will do for your relationship.

Intimacy is crucial between two people when part of a couple, especially in the bedroom. Intimacy is what brings you close and keeps you close. Firstly, we will look at what intimacy means and the different types of intimacy that exist. There are different types of intimacy, and here I will outline them for you before digging deeper into the intimacy between couples. Intimacy, in a general sense, is defined as mutual openness and vulnerability between two people. Therefore, it is not only reserved for romantic relationships. Intimacy can also be present in other types of close relationships like friendships or family relationships. Below, I will outline the different forms of intimacy.

Emotional Intimacy

Emotional intimacy is the ability to express oneself maturely and openly, leading to a deeply personal connection between people. It is also the ability to respond maturely and openly when someone expresses themselves to you by saying things like "I'm sorry" or "I love you too." This open and vulnerable dialogue leads to an emotional connection. There must be a mutual willingness to be vulnerable and honest, with more in-depth thoughts and feelings for a deep personal connection to form. This is where this type of emotional intimacy comes from.

Intellectual Intimacy

Intellectual intimacy is a kind of intimacy that involves discussing and sharing thoughts and opinions on intellectual matters. They gain fulfillment and feelings of closeness with the other person. For example, if you discuss politics with someone you deem to be an intellectual equal, you may find that you feel a closeness with them as you share your thoughts and opinions and connect on an intellectual level. Many people find intellect and brains to be sexy in a partner!

Shared Interests and Activities

This form of intimacy is less well-known, but it is also considered a form of intimacy. When you share activities with another person, you both enjoy and are passionate about it. This creates a sense of connection. For example, when you cook together or travel together. These shared experiences give you memories to share, leading to bonding and intimacy (openness and vulnerability). This type of connection is usually present in friendships, familial relationships, and, more importantly, in romantic relationships. Being able to share interests and activities leads to a closeness that can be defined as intimacy.

Physical Intimacy

Physical intimacy is what most people think of when they hear the term "intimacy," as it is the type of intimacy that includes sex and all activities related to sex. It also involves other non-sexual types of physical contact, such as hugging and kissing. Physical intimacy can be found in close friendships or familial relationships where hugging and kisses on the cheek are common, but it is most often found in romantic relationships.

Physical intimacy is the type of intimacy involved when people are trying to make each other orgasm. Physical intimacy is almost always required for orgasm. Physical intimacy doesn't necessarily mean that you are in love with the person you are having sex with; it just means that you are doing something intimate with another person physically.

It is also possible to be intimate with yourself. While this begins with the emotional intimacy of self-awareness, it also involves the physical closeness of masturbation and physical self-exploration. I define sexual, the physical intimacy of the self as being in touch with the parts of yourself physically that you would not usually be in touch with if you are a woman, your breasts, clitoris, vagina, and anus. Suppose you are a man, your testicles, your penis, your anus. Being physically intimate with yourself allows you to have more fulfilling sex, more fulfilling orgasms, and a more fulfilling overall relationship with your body. Being in charge of your own body while it is in another person's hands is very important. This is why masturbation is such a pivotal element to physical intimacy.

CHAPTER 4:

Finance

Money-it's probably a couple's most challenging subject to discuss calmly. It is often identified as the leading cause of marital discord. Pairs with an unbalanced perception of this product will suffer from tension, conflict, and emotional damage. However, parents who are unable to overcome money issues friendly also raise children with irrational financial attitudes. But is money meant to cause inconsistencies in your home? Not necessary. Not necessarily. On the contrary, money discussions can strengthen your marriage bond. It's all about how you look at money and how you talk to your spouse about it. Why is money a source of peace and marriage at once?

Many conflicts involving money in the home frequently rely instead of cash or credit on trust or fear. For instance, a husband who demands his wife to account for every hundred she spends may say that he fears that the woman can handle family finances. Likewise, the wife, who worries that her husband saves too little, may express her fear that a future event may cause financial harm to her family. Then there's another challenge-the background of the couple. Consider the hypothetical husband I'm going to call Johnny. He is from a family where his dad was an alcoholic and a smoking band. The dad was often out of work for long stretches. As a result, the family often had to deal with simple things in the house. Based on that background, Johnny developed a real fear of debt or cash flow. Sometimes this fear makes him irrational about money matters with his wife. The wife is from a family, on the other hand, where money was well handled. Of course, she doesn't have the many hang-ups Johnny has about money. Often these gaps lead to tensions.

Learn to Talk calmly about Money

At such moments, emotions would be substantial, making peaceful and constructive conversations almost impossible. This can common the disputes arising from hot emotions and incomprehension. And what can you talk about? Why don't you trust your wife how your parents' attitude to the money could have influenced you? Try to understand how your partner's background could have affected her or his philosophy that one regard. Such discussions may seem awkward, going to depend on the personality of yours and the environment. But if it contributes to home peace, won't you confront it?

Agree as to how Income Is to Be considered

If both you and your spouse earn money, be careful not to claim individual independence. In the family, it does not promote peace. Honor each other by revealing your income and significant expenses. Hiding your income or your high costs can undermine your confidence and harm your relationship. This doesn't mean you have to ask your friend before you pay for a bottle of soda. That could threaten the precious independence that every individual wants reasonably. Yet you illustrate that by reporting larger purchases, you respect your partner and his opinion. In this regard, both of you can agree on an amount each of you can spend without informing the other, whether this is $20, $200, or any other figure. And always ask your partner if you want to spend more than that.

Try Budgeting

It also helps to erase suspicions that either partner has wasted unnecessary money. Facts and figures are difficult to argue about. A family budget should not be as complicated as a national budget. A straightforward calculation of a household's total income, a listing of payroll fixed and variable costs, and judgment on what proportion of payment should be saved after bills are paid. Through keeping a list of actual expenses for many months, you can further refine the family budget and equate them with the existing account. Change your lifestyle to keep your family from falling into debt if necessary.

Distribution Roles

Considering each other's strengths and weaknesses, determine who will take care of what responsibility at home. Here, there is no hard and quick rule. The husband takes care of finances in some households, and the wife takes care of this duty in others. This is what works for your family. The goal is that both you and your partner work as a team (for you!). Besides, you may agree to swap roles sometimes, to learn better what each other does.

Your money conversations don't have to stifle one another's passion. Open discussions on money may be between husband and wife to enhance the love connection. As couples talk about how they want to spend money, they share their goals and desires and, at the same time, affirm their marriage commitment. They respect each other's opinions and sentiments when they consult each other before making large purchases. If they require the relative freedom to spend a certain amount without consultation, they show mutual trust. These are the characteristics of a genuinely loving relationship. Don't they value more than cash? Why argue?

CHAPTER 5:

Family Structure

Relationships are complicated things, even the relationships that exist between family members. To have the best possible relationship with your spouse, your children, or any other family members, you have to play a constant game of trial and error to find out what doesn't work and what does. Over time, relationships grow more substantial, and when you make mistakes, you learn valuable lessons.

All about Family Relationships

The most important part of a healthy family is the relationships that exist between each of the members. Because of these distractions, you may have grown comfortable living in solitude, although the rest of your family shares the same home with you. In fact, for some families, they first have to go through horrible events like accidents or divorce before they realize how meaningful their relationships are.

Learn how to prioritize and nurture your relationships to make them stronger. When this improvement in relationships starts with you, the rest of your family members will also feel encouraged to follow suit. Soon, you will realize that your family has grown closer, and you share more profound relationships. But before you can do this, you should recognize the signs that your family is undergoing problems. To work on making your relationships better, you must deal with existing issues first. Some of the most common issues that cause rifts in your relationships are:

When One Member Has a strong Need for Dominance and Power

Usually, this is felt by one of the parents, although children may feel this too (especially teenagers). All families have dominant members and less dominant members. But if one of the dominant members wants everyone else to follow everything they say, that will cause some tension. For instance, if one of the parents gets involved in a conflict with another family member, it might upset them. When this happens, the parent might exert his control and power by ordering everyone else to cut-off communications with that family member. Naturally, if the family member involved is close to the rest of the family, they might not want to cut-off communication.

If you have one such member in your family, you should have a conversation with them.

When One Family Member Makes Others Feel exhausted

Certain people can make others feel depleted or exhausted, even without trying too hard. For instance, if your spouse finds parenting too tricky, and they become incredibly pessimistic.

Even the smallest things set them off, and they end up taking out their frustrations on you or, worse, on your children. This is another issue that you have to deal with first before starting your minimalist journey.

Lack of Loyalty

Sometimes, when family issues get too overwhelming, one spouse tries to find comfort in another person instead of dealing with the home issues. Lack of loyalty may also manifest when a teenager chooses their friends or boy/girlfriend over their family.

Generally, though, a lack of loyalty happens because there is also a lack of communication between family members. Be brave enough to reach out, especially when you feel like an issue is troubling one of your family members. Loyalty doesn't just happen — you should love and nurture each other so that you will all feel loyalty and trust towards each other no matter what challenges come your way.

Financial Issues

Fortunately, this is one problem that you can deal with through minimalism. When you focus on material things (including money), it won't be that much of a problem anymore.

Abusive Family Members

Sadly, so many people have been abused physically, emotionally, verbally, or psychologically by their family members. The effects of abuse don't go away smoothly, and some even carry the repercussions of these experiences until they grow up. If needed, ask for professional help to deal with this issue.

CHAPTER 6:

Parenting

Parenting is a game-changer to all marriages. In many ways, it can change the relationship dynamic for the better or worse, depending on the specific set of circumstances. In television commercials featuring baby-shower cards, diapers, and a litany of baby products, parenting and marriage are depicted as pure bliss and effortless. Your relatives will sell you a story about how babies are a heaven-sent bundle of happiness — and they are — but they skip the hard work that goes into making it all work! Of course, it is essential to love our children. But it is crucial to be alive to what parenting does to marriages. There is no reason that loving your child and working on your marriage should be mutually exclusive. A happy marriage almost always means a happy baby. Marriage happiness, sustainability, and worth are liked at the hip with parenting.

Can Parenting Be Used to Strength Marriages?

It is not easy. It is difficult. But marriage can be used to sweeten your marriage, make it more robust and long-lasting! Most people view parenting as a collection of stressors that will make your life miserable and probably accelerate the end of your relationship with your spouse. However, with the right touch, parenting can be the glue that holds you together. In this regard, it will benefit your relationship and the well-being of the kid(s).

All you can do to leverage parenting in improving your relationship within a marriage is to put your relationship first. Recognizing that your marriage is a work in progress goes a long way to cementing your commitment towards bolstering your bonds. Working on your differences consistently also helps strengthen your relationship's foundations while ironing out disagreements before they become more significant issues.

A focus on appreciating each other while minimizing criticism is essential in sweetening your relationship. Communication is the underlying foundation of a relationship. Maintaining the bidirectional flow of information, opinions, views, and perspectives are necessary, retaining the enthusiasm to sustain a relationship of married spouses with a kid(s).

Using parenting as a tool to improve your relationship quality and sustainability needs a deliberate effort targeting parenting dynamics. Understanding the expected disruptions to the relationship parenting brings will help you be better prepared. It also means that you are better equipped to harness the parenting changes and work for your relationship.

Learning about parenting and preparing for the shifts it brings should include both spouses. This process must be collaborative because both of you will need the knowledge and skills to maneuver through the impending changes. Secondly, a concerted approach is likely to succeed in maintaining a working and significant relationship. When both of you put in the work, you are susceptible to shoulder the burden equitably. Although parenting cannot biologically be equitable, it creates a sense that the husband is supportive of the wife during this period.

The challenge facing most couples going into marriage is that they are not prepared for parenting disruptions. They are not ready for the upending of their lives they face after the baby is born, and parenting begins. As a result, parenting becomes overwhelming, physically, and emotionally. This leads to a surge in conflicts and an increase in the likelihood of divorce or unhappy marriages/relationships.

Use Parenting as a Platform to Build a stronger and long-lasting Relationship and Marriage:

- **Talk About the Certainties and Uncertainties Ahead**

    Talking about uncertainties does not make them any more confident. However, it will help you be emotionally prepared and sure of yourself when navigating through parenting moments and circumstances.

    It is also essential to plan and ventilate some particular issues, such as splitting errands and household chores. It is essential to talk about where the income of the family will come from. In this case, it is crucial to answering the following questions: Who will be the breadwinner? And who is going to stay at home rearing the child?

Talk about the day-care option. Establish who will get your baby to the day-care center and who will get him/her back. Explore the issue of a babysitter, the budget for this option, and plan your lives around what you agree. Figure out how night shift duties will be split, who will wash or sterilize the breast pump and bottles daily. Figure out the shopping schedule, cooking plan, and cleaning chores.

These details seem small and harmless. But without figuring out the division of labor regarding these aspects, they might contribute to frustration, stress, and depression. If left unsorted, they can gnaw away at the relationship.

- **Focus on the Downside of Parenthood with the View of Avoiding Its Pitfalls on the Marriage**

Maintaining a positive and hopeful perception of parenting is important for new fathers and mothers. But it is vital to guard against lofty expectations shattered by the reality of fatherhood and motherhood.

Yes, babies offer immense joy, and they bring a lot of happiness to a marriage. They also carry an uptick in physical and emotional exertions that can take their toll on the relationship. Bathing the baby, feeding, entertaining, and changing the baby 24 hours a day and 7 hours a week are demanding chores. All couples should be emotionally and physically prepared for such demands before they begin their roles as parents.

Focusing on and talking about the downside(s) of parenting is essential in marriage. It will help you to cope with the changes and disruptions to your lives. It is okay to talk about your fatigue, frustrations, and even anger with your spouse. Ensure, to be honest with your partner regarding these issues and also maintaining a supportive stance.

Feeling anger, frustration, and fatigue does not mean that you are a terrible parent. It is crucial to admit these emotions and focus on working together to resolve them within the marriage. This approach helps in disarming these emotions and thus prevents them from negatively affecting your relationship.

- **Maintain Honesty about Gains and Losses**

In many instances, parenting will lead to some gains and losses. For example, you have gained the baby of your dreams. He/she melts your heart every time you see them. However, you cannot avoid feeling sad and empty because of the loss of your typical sex life. For the mother, you lost your sleek pre-baby size 8s and replaced them with elastic-waist jeans.

Most new parents typically complain, silently, about the disruption to their lives occasioned by the baby and their parenting duties and responsibilities. These complaints and silent resentment cause the marital distance to widen. In some extreme instances, it can lead to shame and a decline in self-esteem.

For example, a new daddy might feel replaced by the baby in his spouse's life and affection. The mother might be frustrated and even sad about how parenting (pregnancy, nursing, and the rigors of childcare) has transformed her body. These feelings are normal among new parents.

Sharing such feelings of loss, shame, or disruption is vital in dealing with parenting's emotional toll. Maintaining honesty about these issues with your partner helps you to feel better and strengthen your bond as a couple.

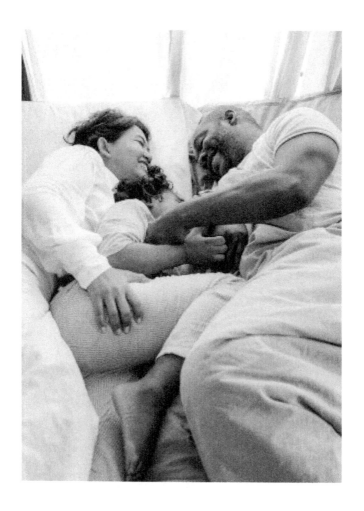

CHAPTER 7:

Extended Family

In-Laws Controversies

Much of the families struggle with in-law's issues at some stage. First, you might believe your in-laws are not helping you, or your spouse is too insensitive. So, they have a view about all the things that go of where you're living and how you feed your kids. Getting disputes with in-laws of yours does not imply you are part of an unhealthy relationship. It's analogous to fighting. The controversy should not spoil a relationship. And somehow, they're likely to do something wrong. But the same goes out for the problems of an in-law. What matters is how they cope with those issues. Here's how equilibrated partners handle their in-laws:

- **Healthy Couples Put Effort to Maintain a good Relationship with Their In-Laws**

They understand the position that their in-laws have in their partner's life. They manage things publicly. They are a component of social roles. They require connections to their families from their in-laws. In certain words, they make an effort, even though they don't generally agree, respect the families' nuances, traditions, or rituals, or even look ahead to the future while being together.

- **Healthy Couples Don't Take It on a personal Basis**

With familiar and complicated human feelings, a happy couple can recognize and deal with the fact that their parents are also human beings. They're trying to figure out where they came from because they are empathizing.

- **Healthy Couples Get to Know Their In-Laws Are Unique People**

Good households deal with their in-laws and recognize that in specific ways, they are unique people.

The communities still have their existence. Good couples realize culture is not wrong or bad, just unique.

- **Healthy Couples Have Their Perfect Boundaries with Their In-Laws**

They should have open conversations with their spouses about their interests and create a plan that they both rely on. For instance: Your partner is okay with an unannounced one coming from his mother. You don't. And you believe you can call family members in advance to make sure it's a fun moment to go over.

- **Healthy Couples how to Maintain the Difference between Their Spouse and Their In-Laws**

Mom can be disrespectful and critical of an individual, for example. Still, a successful couple understands that her behavior does not portray how the guy feels about the items she focuses on.

- **Healthy Couples Distinct Their Relationship from Their In-Laws**

As they're not partnering with them, regardless of how complicated or disagreeable their in-laws can be. Though the in-laws are incredibly challenging to deal with, satisfied individuals give their partner a particular opportunity to succeed. They can say, "I love you" or perform a sweet gesture.

- **Healthy Couples Know how to Maintain Their Communication**

To deal with in-laws is term sorting. Therefore, they dream about their places.

They are careful. They have complete respect for each other's feelings.

Tips for Dealing with In-Laws

Five more guidelines for coping with the in-laws are here:

- **Setting Your Boundaries**

  Defines the boundaries that you wish to arrange for your in-laws. For example, if your mother-in-law takes over your kitchen every time she comes, talk about it to your spouse. Then talk with her about this same problem in a polite but still straightforward manner.

- **Take deep Breaths for Getting Relax**

  Take a break to relax while you're about to hit a breakpoint. Find a quiet spot, like a shower room, or have a walk. When relaxing, reflect on your in-law's good qualities, such as just enjoying our family, also note that you cannot influence them or alter them.

Your in-laws and they are part of your life, are meaningful to your family. It is up to all of you to find a way to make the time with extended family as fun as possible.

- **Remember Your In-Laws Are People**

They are like you. They have interests, fears, anxieties, and thoughts. Do not treat them as caretakers, just like every other person you slowly become familiar with.

- **Remember, It's Just an Opinion**

If your mother-in-law recommends feeding your child with a different diet, take note that you don't have to accept it, defend it out of the presence or view it as your criticism. Although we can't help but speak with an in-law, we can legislate how we hear them.

- **Respect Your Spouse's Attachments**

As it helps to view the husband's commitment to his relatives as something that should be valued.

For starters, if your husband's regular calls to his father are worth able to him, then recognizing and acknowledging that is valuable to you.

CHAPTER 8:

Build Trust

Fidelity in a marriage isn't just sexual; it's emotional, physical, psychological, and spiritual. When you trust your marriage partner, you are saying I can trust who you are. It means that you respect and understand your partner's actions and decisions, that you believe your partner is reliable in their word and predictably safe in their choices. Trust is the ability to coexist peacefully with the unknown and act with incomplete information because you've filled in the gaps with tacit knowledge that feels safe, intimate, and understandable.

Trust requires a mystical blend of intimate knowledge of another person, and a willingness to accept that another person can never fully, wholly be known. In marriage, trust is an essential ingredient for success. Breaches of trust are like holes in the bottom of a boat: Whether the water seeps in through hundreds of tiny rot spots or gushes through one gaping hole, without repair, that boat is going to sink. (But you could always decide to get on another boat together!)

Build Trust with Time-Outs

Despite your best intentions, the train of communication will still derail. Sometimes it's a spectacular crash; other times, you feel the wheels start to rattle, and you know to slow down.

That's what a time-out does — it slows things down so that you can both get back on the track of connection, mutual understanding, and alignment. Pausing a problematic conversation is also a way to build and maintain trust in your marriage.

It says to your partner, "What we're talking about is important, but I'm having trouble listening with my heart. Trust me to take a break and come back when I'm ready."

Here Are the Step-by-Step Do's and Don'ts of Taking a Time-Out:

a. **Frame the Need for a Time-Out in Terms of Your Own Experience, Rather than Blaming Your Partner**

- Don't blame your partner by saying something like, "You're getting worked up. Have a break to calm down."

- Do acknowledge the helpfulness of a time-out for yourself. For example: "I'm feeling overwhelmed. What you're saying is important, but I'm having trouble listening to what you're saying. I need a break, and then we can try again."

b. **Engage in healthy Self-soothing**

- Don't numb or escalate (that is, don't avoid or minimize your feelings, use substances, shame or blame yourself for needing a break, complain to others, or shut down).

- Do relax and recover. For example, meditate, take a shower or a bath, exercise, or go for a walk, write in a journal, read, or watch a funny TV show.

c. **Revisit the Conversation in Your Mind to Prepare for another Try**

- Don't skip this step. Couples who only self-soothe but don't engage in the work of perspective-taking end up rehashing the same fight over and over again. Time-outs are helpful only if you both identify ways you can do better after. Recovery takes active processing.

- Do remember what is essential. Couples are ready to try again for a productive conversation when they've spent the time-out actively processing what happened. What's important is that you're a team, you speak and listen with your heart, and you prevent further damage. Ask yourself questions like, "When I felt triggered, what did I think my partner was trying to say or intending to mean? What triggered my partner? How do I imagine they felt? How can I state my needs differently so my partner can hear me? How can I convey that I understand where my partner is coming from, even if I disagree?"

d. **Try Again**

- Don't assume that you don't need to talk about the conflict because you're feeling better from self-soothing and active processing. Honor the request to try again, and give yourselves the chance to get back to the original issue.

- Do return to the conversation when you're both ready. Bring a more intentional awareness of the skills you've learned, like active listening (see here) or Stop, Drop, Swap (see here). And add in some physical touching this time — remember, it's harder to argue when you're touching!

e. **Interacting with each other during the Time-Out**

You may still need to interact with each other during the break from your difficult conversation. Perhaps you need to get the kids to bed during the time-out or meet friends for brunch. How should you interact with each other during the in-between time? Remember, the time-out is meant to repair a communication derailment, not to do further damage. You can be warm and not ready to talk about the issue at hand. You can process hurt feelings and not punish your partner.

• Don't be passive-aggressive, cold, distant, or sarcastic; don't slam doors or sigh heavily.

• Do be respectful, warm, friendly, and kind; maintain small acts of affection, and smile.

Betrayals

Betrayals in marriage take many forms, from affairs to secrets to lies. At its core, a betrayal is a form of disloyalty — an indication that something or someone else has taken

THE MARRIAGE COUNSELING WORKBOOK

priority, preference, or value over the partnership. Betrayal in a marriage is toxic because it signals violations of marriage values like mutuality, respect, and teamwork. Two of the most common forms of betrayal in marriage, besides sexual betrayals, are secrets and lies.

Secrets

Secrets in a marriage can take different forms — perhaps you've started withholding information to avoid a conflict, like when you use cash to pay for something, so there isn't a credit card trail.

Or perhaps you're keeping secrets from your partner because you're ashamed of the truth (or what your partner would think about your truth), like when you bought a pack of cigarettes even though you're trying to quit and your partner would be disappointed.

Marriage asks us to be vulnerable and open with our partner and requires us to do our part to create an emotionally safe environment that facilitates such sharing. It asks of one another, "Share your true self with me."

66 | P a g .

Lies

Consistency and honesty are two fundamental values in a partnership. To build lives together, you need to know that your partner will do what they say and say what they mean, and vice versa. Intentional deception quickly undermines trust in a marriage, no matter if the lies are "white" or "whoppers." Like why we might keep a secret from our partner, a lie can be a way to avoid confrontation. "I didn't tell you because I knew you'd get upset — just like you're doing now!" But lying only compounds the injury; one wound is the complicated truth itself, and the other is the deception that hid that truth. Even those dealing with betrayal on the affair level often hear from my clients that the lying hurts more than the actions.

CHAPTER 9:

Roles and Expectation

You should believe that your partner does not fulfill your emotional needs. However, marriage counselors and psychologists usually believe that only you can satisfy these needs.

It's not meant to be seen as a hollow emotional container packed with your partner. You've got to take responsibility for your results. The best way to do this is to recognize and fulfill the needs of your partner first.

To Meet What Your Spouse Needs

Both men and women have very different needs. Learning to consider and fulfill your partner's needs can be difficult, but it is vital to creating a successful marriage. If the adversary is granted a foothold, it will devastate a few purely because of their unmet needs and desires.

In a variety of instances, married couples tend to struggle to fulfill their partners' needs. Satisfying your emotional desires requires putting the needs of your partner ahead of your own.

Having a proper understanding of your partner's emotional needs is one of the keys to success in a long-term, engaged relationship. Not meeting all of your partner's needs is not your responsibility.

If you want your spouse to take action to meet your needs magically, you are asking for them to change.

Instead, be direct and frank to your partner. Ask what you need. Would you like change, understanding, or compatibility? Whatever you need, requesting it directly will significantly improve your chances of getting it.

Show Your Spouse that You Care

This is where the need for reciprocity comes into play. Time and again, show your spouse that you appreciate and care for them. Reminding your partner that you know your life is better because they are in is very motivating and loving.

Kindness Goes a long Way

It doesn't matter what the act of kindness is. The vital thing is that your spouse knows that they are valued, that you know what they want and need, and that you are willing to provide it without prompting.

These efforts to learn and offer are the keys to a successful marriage and relationship, and eventually, fulfill your own needs.

Take Responsibility for Yourself

Understand that you are in a relationship to bond with your spouse, share events large or small, and build a life together. Prepare for disappointment since both parties cannot always satisfy each other. Expecting another person to meet our needs entirely is asking too much of anyone.

Expectations are grueling that all humans are fallible and have their wants and needs. This is unlikely to change in your own space or that of anyone else.

Don't see where your spouse needs to change. Look where you need to change. Don't have expectations of your spouse. In case you have expectations, wear it on.

If your partner knows that you care about her and that she is there to help her with big and small things, they are much more likely to reciprocate. Fulfilling your emotional needs begins with sharing and caring for your partner. A person who feels loved, cared for, and valued is much more likely to reciprocate in kind.

CHAPTER 10:

Society and Culture

The best-case scenario is when all of your friends and the friends of your partner love you as much as they love your mate. It will happen occasionally but rarely is it proper for every friend and every situation. Friends might begin to wonder why your time is being taken up so much with your partner, especially if they are not in a relationship. Friends and Friction

Relationships evolve out of the desire for partners to spend increasing amounts of time around one another, often forgoing anyone else's presence. It can seem like a shock to friends used to spending all of the time they want at your residence or out doing favorite activities. You suddenly have less time available, which can strike feelings of insecurity, loneliness, or abandonment by close friends. It's essential to allow them to feel included at times, but you also need to give your partner the healthiest part of your time. If the feelings of resentment and insecurity aren't too drastic, it's a situation that can work when you make the right moves.

Leaving Childhood Friends Behind — Is It necessary

You have to draw a figurative line in the sand for intolerable behaviors. You need to stay in close communication with your partner concerning how friends are treating you and them. You might want to consider a calm confrontation or begin cutting ties if:

- Friends begin to make crude remarks or sexual advances towards your partner.

- Friends are hostile towards you or your partner.

- They bring constant negativity.

- They make increasing demands on your time.

- They tell lies to your partner to try and make them angry towards you.

You might be able to salvage the situation if you have an open and honest discussion with friends about destructive behaviors, but there are times that friendships have to go if you want to stay with your chosen partner.

Eliminating the Third-Wheel Syndrome

Try being more low-key about any plans you have if you find friends suddenly showing up at the same restaurants or events and inviting themselves to hang out. Nothing seems more miserable on a date night than having an unexpected and unwanted third-wheel.

You can offer to do a double-date if they want to plan ahead of time, and comfortable for your partner.

You will eventually have to begin being somewhat secretive of unique plans with individuals that won't take a subtle hint. Make sure that schedule some time to spend with them on down the line. You don't want your friends to feel you have completely forgotten about them.

Why Can't Everyone Just Get Along?

Personality clashes can also be a huge problem that makes it nearly impossible to be around their friends or have your partner around your friends. It's rarely a group of individuals. You might have one that lets you continuously know how much they can't stand your mate. Unless the friend begins to modify their language and behavior, the friendships tend to fade off. If they genuinely can't stand you or your partner, they will begin to wean themselves away from your presence. It generally is a problem that takes care of itself.

Making Peace with Bffs

Best friends forever. How often have you heard that term? It's worth taking the time to try and work the situation out if it's a friend you or your partner has great affection for and have maintained a long friendship. Do your best to make your partner's friends feel welcome and included inappropriate events. Avoid rolling your eyes, sighing, or making negative comments when they are around. Remember them on holidays and for their birthday.

Little steps like this can begin to endear you to them, and you'll find their doubts fade away. It eases all manners of insecurity if you keep an open dialogue and demonstrate your care for your partner.

Don't Drag Friends in on Relationship Troubles

Do your level best to not drag friends in on relationship problems. What could be a simple misunderstanding or temporary problem can be blown out of proportion by overly-concerned friends. It forces them to stick with loyalties and makes it unfair to your partner. It can change the dynamics of their interactions and make everyone feel uncomfortable. You can never be sure if your problems aren't being broadcast across town. Relationship problems are never made better through gossip and conjecture. It can deeply hurt the one you love to hear rumors. If you need to confide in a friend, try and follow these rules:

- Make sure it's a friend you trust.

- Keep it as a generalized question, if possible.

- Never heap all of the blame on your partner.

- Make it understood you are looking for a solution, not to end the relationship.

Reserve Time for Friends and Your Partner

Balancing your free time is the crucial component to making friends and your partner happy. Check ahead with your mate to make sure it's okay to go ahead and make plans to see a movie or head out to a basketball game. Encourage your partner to try and find time to spend with their friends occasionally. Having interests outside the relationship helps keep the growth continuing. To make it possible:

- Make sure your partner has met and is comfortable with the friend you will be hanging out with occasionally.

- Make these outings a reasonable amount and length of time.

- Never cancel plans with your partner to spend time with your friends.

- Give priority days and times to your partner. Maintain the traditions and rituals you've started to create.

Conclusion

You know other married couples. Now, every marriage has its problems. A healthy, conscious couple will still say things they regret to each other. They will have many of the same problems you do.

The difference is that a healthy, conscious couple approaches each disagreement one at a time and comes to a plan of action after a conversation in which both parties feel heard.

To let this happen in your relationship involves setting healthy boundaries and acknowledging and then discussing your differences and disagreements openly. Having a good time together doesn't have to be a chore. It just has to be what you have time to give each other.

Becoming more like this couple is only a matter of emulating this strategy.

So, let's break down all the things this conscious marriage gets right. There are two main parts to this couple's success: problem-solving and communication. Since it always has to come first, we will go into communication first.

You have learned a ton of communication skills and concepts that will help you as you try to express more effectively with your partner. Now, dialectical behavior therapy works the same fundamental way for communication and problem-solving: we deal with one issue at a time.

We don't allow ourselves to do any more than that, because otherwise we will be overwhelmed, and we might as well not communicate at all if we aren't doing it well.

One issue at a time also means each spouse takes turns speaking. When one spouse is talking, the other does not interrupt. All they do is listen. You can nod your head and make eye contact with them to show them that you are really listening to them and not just waiting until your turn to talk.

Before I delve into some other critical points in good communication between a married couple, I would like the two of you to discuss what you think it looks like when a married couple can communicate well. You can think back to a couple of you know who does this effectively, although that might be hard to do because couples don't tend to have these difficult conversations around other people.

Thankfully, you probably have at least some examples of times when the two of you managed to communicate well in a difficult situation. Maybe not everything went perfectly. But you can look back on this example and ask yourselves what went right in that particular instance. You can use it as an example for yourselves for the future so you can communicate more like you did that time.

The other primary way you can practice good communication for a relationship is by using "I" statements and working on all four forms of non-verbal communication: eye contact, body language, emotion, and voice. The more aware you are of all of these, the better you will be at tapping into what makes your spouse tick without upsetting them.

You already have a lot to go off of for what will help you communicate better. As long as you have been doing all the exercises along the way, you are even getting integral practice for improving your relationship communication skills.

Then, there is the other side of what makes a marriage work, and that is problem-solving. You can problem-solve already with your spouse, or else you wouldn't be together right now. However, all of us could improve our problem-solving skills, both inside and outside of our relationships.

As you did for the communication part, I would like to ask both of you to take a moment to discuss what makes for good problem-solving skills. Think back to all the scenarios and ideas we have already gone through to help your thoughts flow. Whatever you come up with, coming up with ideas will be a fruitful way to hone practical communication skills.

The two of you should now think of a time when there was a difficult problem, and you worked it out together. As you have probably realized, problem-solving and communication are positively related things, so they can be hard to separate. But still, you should try to think of a time when the problem was complicated, specifically, not just when you were able to communicate well.

Financial problems can be significant for finding this kind of example. When we go through rough patches with money and have to find places to cut corners, we have to be inventive sometimes and figure out what we will do differently to make sure we are paying our bills.

The answer to problem-solving is always to work through one thing at a time, even when it is tempting to work on many things at once. When confronted with so many problems, we want to force them to work out at once, but life doesn't work that way. Do your best to have just one problem on your mind that you want to work through, and the rest will follow from there.

Another major part of problem-solving is being humble enough to seek out outside help when you need it. If you are too proud to say to an expert, you need help. You are just dragging out your difficulties much longer than they need to drag out.

Men, in particular, tend to have a problem with asking for outside help. They want to have the appearance of always having things all put together, so they can't risk that facade by showing they can't do everything alone by asking for help.

But on the contrary, if you know you are a man who does this, seeking outside help will only make you seem more reasonable. It shows that you care more about figuring out the problem than preserving your pride.

When it comes to problem-solving, you have to know when to keep working through something and walk away. Working hard is a virtue, but hurting yourself by straining yourself on a difficult task isn't always the answer. We can't always solve things with sheer force.

But we can build habits of motivation so that when a seemingly impossible task becomes apparent, we set our sights on something better. I'm not saying we have to be perfect.

Every once in a while, we need to give ourselves a break and approach a new challenge with a positive attitude.

Sometimes, our best option is to walk away from it for a while and come back after.

Finally, knowing that what makes marriage work is an effective combination of productive communication and good problem-solving. A couple who has both of these things will still have hard times as everyone does, but the difference is, they will feel equipped to deal with that when it happens. You and your spouse gain the potential to get there if you both put in the work.